The Illuminated Manuscript

nfixus sum in limo profundi: & non est
substantia.

eni in altitudinem maris: & tempestas
demersit me.

aboraui clamans rauce facte sunt fau
ces mee: defecerunt oculi mei dum spe
ro in deo meo.

ultiplicati sunt sup capillos capitis mei:
qui oderunt me gratis.

onfortati sunt qui psecuti sunt me ini

The Illuminated Manuscript

JANET BACKHOUSE

Phaidon ✦ Oxford

Phaidon Press Limited, Littlegate House, St Ebbe's Street,
Oxford

First published 1979
This edition published by Marboro Books by
 arrangement with Phaidon Press Ltd, 1986
© 1979 Phaidon Press Ltd
All rights reserved

ISBN 0 7148 1969 7
Library of Congress Catalog Card Number: 78-73502

Printed in Singapore by GnP Consultants Pte Ltd

FRONTISPIECE. York Psalter: *The Resurrection; Jonah and
the Whale.* England (diocese of York), about 1250–60.
193 folios. 335 × 240 mm. Additional MS 54179,
folio 59b.

List of Plates

Select Bibliography

The following recent general surveys should be easily accessible. Each of them suggests detailed further reading for the field which it covers.

C. R. Dodwell, *Painting in Europe 800–1200* (Pelican History of Art), Penguin Books 1971.

J. Harthan, *Books of Hours*, Thames and Hudson 1977.

A. Martindale, *The rise of the artist in the Middle Ages and early Renaissance*, Thames and Hudson 1972.

J. Porcher, *French miniatures from illuminated manuscripts*, Collins 1960.

M. J. Rickert, *Painting in Britain: the Middle Ages* (Pelican History of Art), Penguin Books 1954 and 1965.

M. Salmi, *Italian miniatures*, Collins 1957.

Up-to-date surveys are not available for every style and period. Useful, though not exhaustive, bibliographies are given for the appropriate chapters in *The book through 5000 years*, edited by H. D. L. Vervliet, Phaidon 1972.

The Illuminated Manuscript

The seventy manuscripts represented in this book span almost nine hundred years of European art and history. When the Lindisfarne Gospels (Plate 1) was written and illuminated at the end of the seventh century, much of Europe was still honouring heathen gods and the British Isles marked the outer limit of the known world. But when Diogo Homem painted his atlas about 1558 (Plate 69) he was able to record the results of almost seven decades in the exploration of the New World, Europe was in the religious turmoil of Reformation and Counter-Reformation, and a hundred years of printing had already transformed the making and distribution of books.

For most of the intervening period illuminated books are the most important source for our knowledge of the history and development of European painting. Painted decorations on a larger scale, such as murals, mosaics or the colouring of carvings, have been subject not only to the natural wear and tear of time but also to changes in fashion, grand schemes for improvement and, in more recent periods, the over-zealous attentions of well-meaning restorers. Paintings on panel become common only during the latter part of the Middle Ages. The paintings in manuscripts outnumber all these many times over and must, indeed, have done so from the beginning. It is, however, very important never to lose sight of the fact that the miniatures in illuminated books were not conceived as individual and independent paintings. They are book illustrations and are thus always intimately connected with a text. It is often only through the thorough examination of this text that their subjects can be correctly understood, and they should never be thought of except in the context and on the scale of the page. A single illuminated book may contain several hundred paintings. In spite of loss and damage, and of the inevitable variations in standard between one book and another, especially those representing the later and more commercialized periods of production, hundreds of thousands of miniatures of the very highest excellence have survived. Many of those in public collections are still unfamiliar even to specialists, and even today the occasional important and completely unknown manuscript is still emerging from private hands. Our seventy plates all come from manuscripts in the British Library, which has one of the largest collections in the world. This selection could be multiplied many times over from the British Library alone, and several other great libraries could without difficulty produce their own lists of equal variety and richness.

The preparation of an illuminated book has always been a very expensive business. The pages are almost invariably made out of vellum. Although paper, originally an oriental invention, was known in Europe quite early

7

in the Middle Ages, it was not produced there in large quantities until the early fifteenth century. Its full development really coincides with the development of printing. It was neither fine enough in finish nor sufficiently durable to be attractive to illuminators and only one, very late, example among our plates (Plate 66) is a paper book. Vellum was usually prepared from the skins of sheep or calves and the size of the animal governed the maximum size of book which could be made. Each double sheet of one of the great Carolingian or Romanesque Bibles represents one animal, so that a single one of these volumes may be thought of as a flock of between two and three hundred sheep. Several pages for a smaller book would of course be cut from one skin. The vellum used for the tiny Bibles typical of the thirteenth century and for some of the late Books of Hours is of such fine quality that it feels almost like tissue paper, and this was probably made from the skins of very young animals.

Ink was prepared either from carbon (fine soot or lamp-black) or from iron-gall (sulphate of iron and oak apples) combined with gum and water. The former produces a permanent black and the latter a brownish tint. Coloured pigments were made from many substances, animal, vegetable and mineral. Some of these were commonly accessible in most parts of Europe but others travelled thousands of miles along the international trade routes from countries which were themselves on the brink of legend. One of the most exotic of the minerals is lapis lazuli, from which the finest deep-blue pigment is made. The sole source of this was Afghanistan and the mines there were described by Marco Polo, who visited them at the end of the thirteenth century. It was, however, used six centuries earlier by the artist of the Lindisfarne Gospels, who must have been unaware of the very existence of the land from which it came. Gold in manu-

scripts, as elsewhere, indicated wealth and status. It could be applied in two main ways, either ground to powder and mixed into a paint, which leaves a somewhat granular surface, or beaten into leaf and laid over a prepared adhesive ground, after which it would be burnished and perhaps additionally embellished with punch marks or tooling.

Stout wooden boards covered with leather were used for the bindings of most manuscripts. The leather might itself be decorated with tooling. Many of the great liturgical manuscripts, designed for public use, were additionally embellished with gold, jewels and enamels, matching the splendour of the altar vessels. Later books made for private owners, especially Book of Hours, were often covered in brightly coloured silk, velvet or brocade and might have gold or jewelled clasps.

The popular belief that all manuscripts were made by monks, toiling away for the glory of God in draughty Gothic cloisters, is more or less true of the early Middle Ages but very far from accurate from the thirteenth century onwards. At the beginning of the Middle Ages the monasteries were the principal centres of learning and culture, and they often provided such education as was available for young men of good family. The monastic communities were themselves the chief customers for fine books, both those intended to provide the reading matter enjoined by the Rule of St Benedict and those designed as part of the furnishing of their churches. Books in the latter class reflected the piety and standing both of the community and of its secular benefactors, and most of the greatest manuscripts of the early Middle Ages fall within it. Specialists amongst the monks themselves learnt the skills necessary to provide the books and a community lacking these skills, or perhaps only newly-founded, might apply to another monastery for essential books to be made. Some abbeys, such as Echternach (see Plate 11), apparently fulfilled outside orders on a very large scale at certain periods of their early history. Even as early as the eleventh century, however, there is evidence of the existence of artists who were not members of religious communities but who made their livings where and when their services were needed. It should be understood that in medieval eyes an artist was simply a craftsman, his activities having little to do with the twentieth-century notions of self-expression, individual genius and 'artistic temperament' that nowadays cling to his profession.

By the beginning of the thirteenth century there had been many changes and developments in society as a whole, very important amongst which for the arts of book production was the foundation of the earliest universities. A more general distribution of wealth at the higher end of the social scale and a gradual increase in the number of people with some claim to literacy led inevitably to a greater demand for books. At this period there begins to be evidence of secular scribes and illuminators living and working amongst other craftsmen in the towns and eventually, like them, forming their own craftsmen's guilds. Sometimes, unfinished manuscripts offer special insights into their working methods, revealing how the writing and decoration of a single book might be divided between a number of hands. In later centuries the most fashionable workshops quite clearly employed many illuminators, only the best of whom painted miniatures, and these workshops must have compiled some form of collective pattern book, so that the same subjects could be repeated again and again to order.

The monastic production of books did not, of course, suddenly cease. It seems not unlikely that some religious communities themselves may have made manuscripts on a commercial basis. The large numbers of books attributed to thirteenth-century St Albans must have cost a very great deal in materials alone and can hardly have been made entirely for love.

The gradual change in market was reflected in a corresponding change in emphasis in the types of book commonly produced. Fine liturgical books for public worship were still of course made, but liturgical books for personal use, such as the Psalter and the Book of Hours which was to supersede it, and works of scholarship and literature became more common. The Book of Hours was the greatest medieval and renaissance best-seller and examples survive in their thousands, in almost every library in the world, ranging in quality from the masterpieces made about 1400 for the Duke of Berry, brother of the King of France, to ill-written specimens into which early woodcuts have been pasted in place of painted illustrations. Popular histories, many of them translated from the original Latin into French, which was more or less generally understood by the upper classes throughout Europe, were provided with cycles of illustration, and so were contemporary literary works in the vernacular, such as Dante's *Divina Commedia*.

Printing with movable types was introduced in Germany by Gutenberg in the middle of the fifteenth century, but its effect upon manuscript-making was far from immediate. During the second half of the fifteenth century the demand for illuminated books was greater than ever before and the products of the time include the early masterpieces of the Flemish workshops. Attention is often drawn to the fact that early printed books look very much like manuscripts, the implication being that the printers were deliberately attempting to make them more acceptable to a market accustomed to hand-written books. There is certainly evidence that some of the great contemporary bibliophiles, such as the Italian Duke of Urbino, disdained to have mass-produced books on their shelves, but this is not the reason for the similarity. Early printed books were bound to resemble manuscripts simply because there was no other model available for them to follow. Only as printing gradually developed in its own right did it become independent in appearance. Nor was there at first any distinction drawn between manuscript and printed book when somebody wanted a copy of a particular text. It was little easier in the late fifteenth century to go out and buy a printed book, unless one happened to live close to the appropriate printer's shop, than it was to order a manuscript copy. There are several examples of a would-be customer apparently borrowing from a friend or neighbour a Caxton edition which particularly interested him and ordering a scribe to make him a copy of it.

By the beginning of the sixteenth century the situation had changed. Printing was already commonplace throughout Europe. Magnificent illuminated manuscripts continued to be made in large numbers in Italy, France and Flanders until well into the middle of the century (Plates 66–8), but they were clearly regarded as luxury items. The printers had appropriated the bottom end of the market. The making of illuminated books has, however, continued on a small scale until the present day, now in one country and now in another. One particularly good but usually overlooked series of fine manuscripts was produced in France in the reign of Louis XIV and is associated with the name of Nicolas Jarry, though other hands certainly contributed. Many of the illuminator's techniques were also adopted by the painters of portrait miniatures, which became fashionable during the sixteenth century. In the nineteenth century, encouraged by the general fashion for things 'Gothic', illuminating became a popular drawing-room art and many manuals of instruction appeared. About eighty years ago a serious revival of interest in the practical aspects of calligraphy and illumination inspired research into medieval and renaissance methods and techniques, which has helped us to a better understanding of some of the masterpieces of earlier centuries.

The Lindisfarne Gospels (Plate 1) is one of the first and greatest masterpieces of medieval European book painting and the names of the craftsmen responsible have come down to us. The scribe and illuminator was Eadfrith, who became Bishop of Lindisfarne in May 698, and the book's earliest binding was provided by Ethilwald, who succeeded him in 721. The manuscript was probably made in honour of the translation of the relics of St Cuthbert (d. 687) in March 698, at which time both men were members of the Lindisfarne monastic community. Its intricate decoration combines motifs inspired by metalwork with complicated patterns made up of birds and beasts. One of the most delightful creatures in the manuscript, a domestic cat, appears on this page, his head and forepaws at the foot of the right-hand margin, gazing hungrily towards a nearby row of interlaced birds.

1. LINDISFARNE GOSPELS: *opening of St Luke*. England (Lindisfarne), about 698. 259 folios. 340 × 250 mm. Cotton MS Nero D. iv, folio 139.

2. VESPASIAN PSALTER: *David and his musicians*. England (Canterbury), second quarter of the eighth century. 160 folios. 235 × 180 mm. Cotton MS Vespasian A. i, folio 30b.

3. HARLEY GOLDEN GOSPELS: *St Matthew*. Carolingian Empire (Aachen), about 800. 208 folios. 365 × 250 mm. Harley MS 2788, folio 13b.

Early Christianity in the north of England had strong Irish foundations. In the south the conversion of the Anglo-Saxons was directly due to the initiative of Pope Gregory the Great, who sent St Augustine from Rome to Canterbury in 597. Augustine brought books with him, and volumes traditionally associated with his name were preserved as relics over the high altar at Canterbury during the later Middle Ages. The Vespasian Psalter (Plate 2) was amongst these, though it dates from the eighth century, long after Augustine's time. The decoration in the border to the miniature is related to native work such as the Lindisfarne Gospels, but the figures are adapted from earlier, more classical sources.

Anglo-Saxon and Irish saints and scholars played a vital role in the conversion of Europe, especially during the seventh and eighth centuries, and through them insular art influenced the work of early continental illuminators. The Frankish ruler Charlemagne, crowned emperor in 800, encouraged learning and the arts throughout his lands, and a series of magnificent Gospels, some of them written entirely in gold, dates from his time (Plate 3). We do not know exactly where these were made, though they may be the products of a workshop attached to his court at Aachen. They do, however, show strong traces of English influence alongside the more obviously classical sources of their figure paintings.

12

4. HARLEY ARATUS: *the constellation Eridanus.* Carolingian Empire (Rheims), mid ninth century. 21 folios. 325 × 280 mm. Harley MS 647, folio 10b (detail).

5. MOUTIERS–GRANDVAL BIBLE: *Moses receiving and transmitting the Law.* Carolingian Empire (Tours), about 840. 449 folios. 510 × 375 mm. Additional MS 10546, folio 25b.

Direct inspiration from a classical source is more easily recognizable in the illustrations of the Harley Aratus (Plate 4). The manuscript contains a Latin translation of the *Phaenomena* of Aratus of Soli, a Greek Stoic philosopher who lived in the third century B.C. This became the fundamental textbook of medieval astronomy, a science of everyday importance, because correct observance of the Church's feast-days depended upon an accurate understanding of the movements of the heavenly bodies. The constellations are portrayed as figures from classical mythology, as they are still today. This Aratus manuscript was later to belong to Canterbury and was copied more than once by English artists.

One of the men most closely associated with Charlemagne in his schemes for the advancement of learning was an English scholar, Alcuin of York (d. 804), whose great achievement was the establishment of a particularly good text of the Latin Bible and who spent the last few years of his life as abbot of Tours. By the middle of the ninth century Tours had become famous as a centre for the production of huge illustrated Bibles using Alcuin's text. The Moutiers–Grandval Bible (Plate 5), which has four full-page miniatures, is one of the earliest surviving examples.

14

... qier danc ielannu cui;
E cmemoref sunc mandacox
ipsiuf adfaciendum ea;

potenci uircuce facien-
cesuerbu illiufadaudien
da uoce sermonum eiuf;

B enedicredno oma opa ei
monu loco dominanonef
ei benedic Anima mea dno;

B CIII· IPSI· O AUTO·
ENEOICANIOO A
mea dno. dne df meuf

tuum; quiambulaf super
pennaf uentozum

stabunc aquae
A bincrepanone ma fugi

6. HARLEY PSALTER: *Psalm* 103, '*Bless the Lord, O my soul*'. England (Canterbury), about 1000. 73 folios. 380 × 315 mm. Harley MS 603, folio 51b (detail).

7. BENEDICTIONAL OF ST ÆTHELWOLD: *the incredulity of St Thomas*. England (Winchester), about 980. 119 folios. 295 × 220 mm. Additional MS 49598, folio 56b.

The Harley Aratus was not the only manuscript to migrate to England in the late tenth century. Outstanding was the Utrecht Psalter (now in Utrecht University Library), in which Carolingian artists had translated the text of the psalms phrase by phrase almost literally into visual form. This manuscript fascinated English artists and it was copied in Canterbury at least three times between its arrival and the end of the twelfth century. In the earliest of these copies, the Harley Psalter (Plate 6), the monochrome drawings of the Carolingian version are translated into a multi-coloured line drawing, which was to become particularly characteristic of late Anglo-Saxon manuscripts.

During the century immediately preceding the Norman Conquest of 1066 English book painting reached a new peak. Manuscripts of this period are collectively assigned to the Winchester School, though Canterbury was also an important centre of production. The masterpiece of the school is the Benedictional made for St Æthelwold, Bishop of Winchester 963–84, by a monk named Godeman (Plate 7). The Benedictional contains the blessings to be pronounced personally by the bishop over his congregation at Mass on feast-days. The more important feasts in Æthelwold's manuscript are marked by miniatures lavishly embellished with gold, twenty-eight of which survive.

16

Picðolice ða iacob þ... he gefeah goðr tuglaſ beþonan hī·he cpæð·
ðir ir goðr fyrō þic· ⁊ he nēðe þðe ſtope naman·manū·þ yr þic ſtop:

Sodlice he ſenðe boðan beþoran hī to eſau hiſ bretþ onſeñ lanðe.
⁊ eþ colmiñ reccað eſauþe mīnū hlaroꝛðe·þ ic þracnoþe mið
labane ⁊ leah hyne oððr ne oðt·Nuic hæbbe oxan ⁊ aſſan ⁊ ſceap
þeoþaſ·⁊ ðeoþena·þic ſtðe ðꝛh ðꝛacan comñ hlaroꝛðe·þ he mīn

8. AELFRIC PENTATEUCH: *Jacob met by angels*. England (Canterbury), second quarter of the eleventh century. 156 folios. 325 × 220 mm. Cotton MS Claudius B. iv, folio 48.

9. LES PRÉAUX GOSPELS: *St Luke*. Normandy, late eleventh century. 169 folios. 275 × 180 mm. Additional MS 11850, folio 91b.

Anglo-Saxon England had the richest tradition of written vernacular literature of any country in Europe, including a large body of original poetry and many translations of earlier Latin works. Among the latter is Ælfric's version of the first five books of the Old Testament, accompanied by about four hundred illustrations (Plate 8). Ælfric had been a pupil of St Æthelwold and was later his biographer. The illustrated copy of his Pentateuch, although it is unfinished and far less polished than the master-pieces of the Winchester School, is of great import-ance for the richness and variety of its subjects.

Manuscripts from eleventh-century Normandy were strongly influenced by contemporary Anglo-Saxon work. The Gospels from the Abbey of Les Préaux (Plate 9) has border decoration closely akin to that in the Benedictional of St Æthelwold (Plate 7), though the figure style is already approaching Romanesque. Normandy had been colonized by the Vikings at the beginning of the tenth century and it is not difficult to see in the Norman invasion of England in 1066, their conquest of Sicily between 1061 and 1091, and their leading role in the First Crusade in 1096, a resurgence of the Viking urge towards expansion and adventure.

18

10. 'ODALRICUS PECCATOR' GOSPEL LECTIONARY: *St Mark*. Ottonian Empire
(?Lorsch), early eleventh century. 75 folios. 205 × 165 mm.
Harley MS 2970, folio 2b.

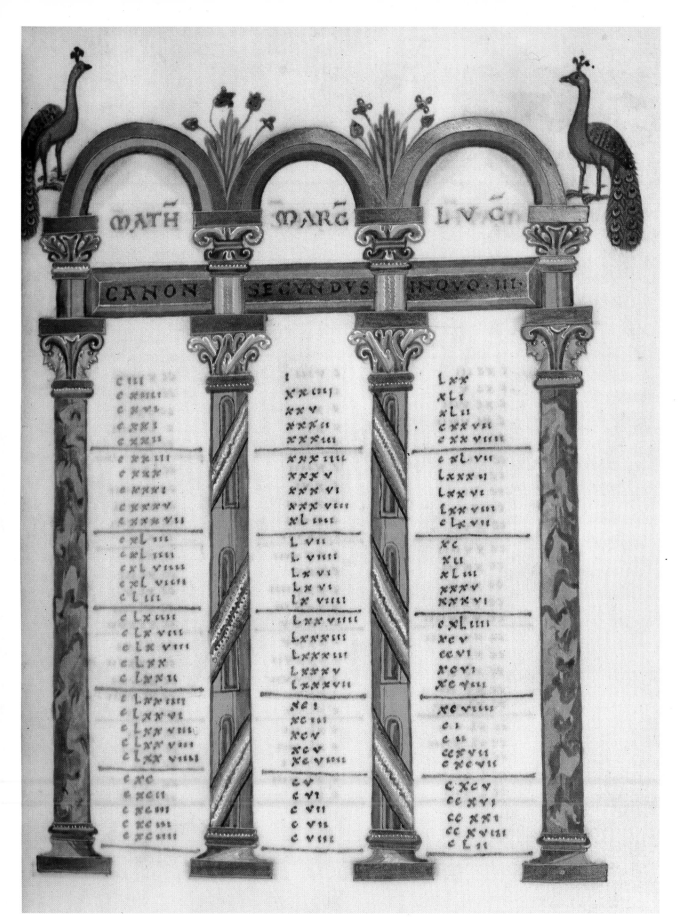

11. GOSPELS: *canon tables*. Ottonian Empire (Echternach), mid eleventh century. 199 folios. 255 × 190 mm. Harley MS 2821, folio 10.

The most magnificent books produced during the tenth and eleventh centuries outside England were made within the German Empire. This school of painting is known as 'Ottonian' because several contemporary emperors were named Otto. Its most significant artist, the Master of the *Registrum Gregorii*, was active towards the end of the tenth century in the service of Egbert, Archbishop of Trier 977–93, and his influence was widespread. One of his followers in southern Germany, perhaps at the Abbey of Lorsch, painted the miniatures in an early eleventh-century Gospel Lectionary (Plate 10), which, in common with several other manuscripts, carries the name of 'Odalricus peccator' ('Ulrich the sinner'). He is presumed to have been the head of the scriptorium in which they were made.

Another leading scriptorium in early eleventh-century Germany was that of the Abbey of Echternach, not far from Trier, where many outstanding manuscripts, some intended for the emperors themselves, were made. Canon tables from one of the smaller Echternach Gospels (Plate 11) demonstrate a characteristic use of colour, with strong emphasis on purple and green. These tables, found in most early copies of the Gospels, represent a system devised in the fourth century whereby parallel passages in the Four Gospels can quickly be located by the reader. Their format naturally inspired elaborate and often ingenious schemes of decoration.

During the early Middle Ages book production in the Italian and Spanish peninsulas stood somewhat apart from the mainstream of European illumination. Comparatively few miniatures of high quality survive from Italy, where style was strongly influenced by Byzantine painting from the eastern Mediterranean, but initial letters in Italian manuscripts are often beautifully decorated with detailed and clear-cut designs. The opening initial of the Camaldoli Psalter is a fine example of this type (Plate 12). The manuscript was made in central Italy, probably at the monastery of Camaldoli where it is known to have been between the thirteenth and the eighteenth centuries.

12. CAMALDOLI PSALTER: '*Beatus*' *initial*. Italy (?Camaldoli), second quarter of the twelfth century. 184 folios. 265 × 190 mm. Yates Thompson MS 40, folio 9b.

Spain was invaded from North Africa at the beginning of the eighth century and much of the country was thereafter under Muslim rule. Islamic influence is clearly recognizable in much early Spanish illumination, the most characteristic vehicles for which were richly illustrated copies of the Commentary on the Apocalypse composed about 776 by the Asturian monk Beatus of Liébana. The Beatus manuscript made at the Abbey of Silos in Castile is one of the later examples, written by 1091 and completed in 1109 (Plate 13).

13. SILOS APOCALYPSE: *the four horsemen*. Spain (Silos), 1109. 280 folios. 380 × 240 mm. Additional MS 11695, folio 102b.

equum fulum.
aequisfedebat
superum abebat
gladium.

equum album
aequisfedebad
superu mabe
bua arcu m

equus niger
aequisfedebat
superum
abebat
staterum.

case aquebatur
cum infernu

equus pallidus
aequisfedebat
superum abebat gladium.

By the middle of the twelfth century manuscripts intended for private use were everywhere becoming more common. The popular book for private worship was the Psalter, to which would usually be added a selection of prayers and a calendar showing the principal feast-days. One such Psalter (Plate 14) was apparently designed for a lady connected with the nunnery at Shaftesbury, then the largest female religious community in England. Its style is linked to that of the St Alban's Psalter (now in Hildesheim), the first great English Romanesque manuscript, which was made before 1123. The Shaftesbury Psalter itself probably dates from the second quarter of the century. It is linked to Shaftesbury by the prominence given in both calendar and litany to St Edward, King and Martyr, who was assassinated in 978 at Corfe at the instigation of his stepmother, so that her own son Ethelred (known to history as the 'Unready') might claim the throne. Edward's relics were translated in the following year to Shaftesbury, and venerated there throughout the Middle Ages. The manuscript is generally thought to have been made somewhere in the southwest of England and it is certainly not impossible that it was made at Shaftesbury itself. Although most Romanesque manuscripts are attributed to communities of monks, the great nunneries must have supported their own scribes and illuminators. It is not clear whether the original owner of the book was a nun or whether she was a lay friend of the abbey. She appears in two of the miniatures in the Psalter, but her simple costume of green veil and brown dress is ambiguous.

14. SHAFTESBURY PSALTER: *the Women at the sepulchre.* England (West Country), about 1130–50. 179 folios. 220 × 130 mm. Lansdowne MS 383, folio 13.

24

Queen Melisende of Jerusalem was the owner of another Psalter of very similar date (Plate 15). In 1131 Melisende succeeded her father, Baldwin II, as ruler of the Latin kingdom which had been established in the Holy Land as a result of the First Crusade and which was to fall before Saladin in 1187. The death of her husband, Fulk of Anjou, in 1143 is not amongst those commemorated in her manuscript's calendar and the book was therefore probably made before it took place. Although the Psalter's miniatures have a very strong Byzantine flavour, study of them makes it clear that this was not native to the artist, even though he signs himself with the Greek name 'Basilius'. The book's arrangement follows western rather than eastern tradition. Three other painters, all rather less skilled than Basilius himself, also worked on the decoration of the manuscript. Such a variety of hands within a single luxury book clearly points to the fact that crusader Jerusalem contained enough potential patrons to support a very substantial scriptorium. Although some of these patrons would have been individuals such as Melisende herself, others were the several religious foundations in and around the city. Melisende's personal foundation was the community of St Lazarus at Bethany, where her younger sister Yvette was installed as abbess. Quite a number of fine liturgical manuscripts made in, and for the use of, the Latin Crusader Kingdoms are to be found in European libraries, having been brought home by the survivors as one by one their strongholds fell.

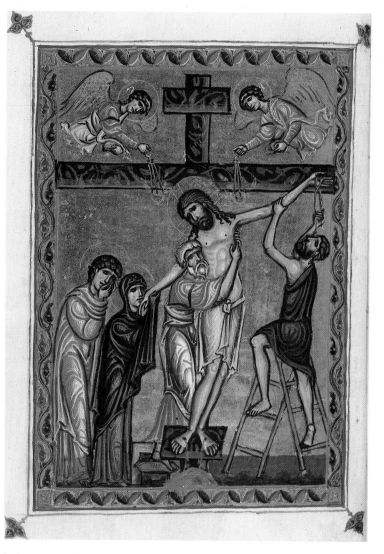

15. QUEEN MELISENDE'S PSALTER: *the descent from the Cross.* Jerusalem, 1131–43. 218 folios. 215 × 140 mm. Egerton MS 1139, folio 8b.

During the first half of the twelfth century the Lower Rhineland and the valley of the Meuse (the 'Mosan' area) became renowned for the achievements of workers in gold and enamels. The Siegburg Lectionary (Plate 16), like other manuscripts produced in the area at that time, bears a marked resemblance to metalwork. Although some of its miniatures are painted in full colour, two are in tinted outline set against panelled backgrounds of the same green and blue that the enamel workers particularly favoured. Siegburg is a monastery about fifteen miles from Cologne and the manuscript contains readings, other than those from the Gospels, for use at Mass on feast-days.

Also carried out in a technique approaching tinted outline rather than in heavy full colour are the miniatures in a Psalter (Plate 17) made at Winchester in the mid twelfth century for the bishop, Henry of Blois (d. 1171), a notable connoisseur and patron of the arts. Henry, a brother of King Stephen, was papal legate to England and when his travels took him to Rome he amazed onlookers by buying antique statues in the market-place there. His Psalter includes thirty-eight pages of pictures from the Old and New Testaments, many of the characters in which are shown in contemporary dress. In this illustration Mary Magdalene, in a long-sleeved gown and with her hair in bound plaits, is seen as a very fashionable young lady.

16. SIEGBURG LECTIONARY: *St Maurice*. Germany (Siegburg), second quarter of the twelfth century. 106 folios. 270 × 160 mm. Harley MS 2889, folio 66b.

17. PSALTER OF HENRY OF BLOIS: *the harrowing of Hell; 'noli me tangere'*. England (Winchester), 1140–60. 142 folios. 325 × 225 mm. Cotton MS Nero C. iv, folio 24.

18. WORMS BIBLE, VOL. I: *the prophet Hosea.* Germany (middle Rhineland), about 1148. 301 folios. 520 × 350 mm. Harley MS 2803, folio 264 (detail).

19. FLOREFFE BIBLE, VOL. II: *the Transfiguration; the Last Supper.* Meuse Valley (Floreffe), about 1156. 256 folios. 480 × 330 mm. Additional MS 17738, folio 4.

QVEM MOYSES VELAT · VOX ECCE PATERNA REVELAT · QVEM EX PROPHETIA REGIT · EST EL IXA MARIA ·:·

hic est fili9 m9 dilectus ·:·

in quo michi complacui ·:·

Nolite timere ·:·

Bonu e nob ee

LEX VETVS IMPLETVR · VBI VERVM PASCHA PARET9 RE: VINVM FIT SANGVIS · CAR9 ... SVBDITVR AGNVS ·:·

20. JOHN THE BAPTIST ROLL: *John cast into prison.* Germany (Alsace), end of the twelfth century. Roll. 870 × 185 mm. Additional MS 42497 (detail).

21. LA CHARITÉ PSALTER: *David and Goliath.* France (La Charité-sur-Loire), end of the twelfth century. 93 folios. 255 × 160 mm. Harley MS 2895, folio 51b (detail).

Enormous Bibles, on the same grand scale as those made at Tours during the ninth century and, like them, designed to be read aloud from a lectern, were a special feature of twelfth-century book production. Examples survive from scriptoria all over Europe. Because of their great weight they are usually bound in more than one volume. Their decoration consists of splendid initials and canon tables, sometimes combined with a few full-page miniatures, and is commonly the work of a team of artists. One fine specimen (Plate 18), the exact provenance of which has yet to be determined, takes its name from Worms Cathedral, to which it belonged in the seventeenth century. It probably

originated somewhere in the Middle Rhineland and was made about 1148. Its style is influenced by both Mosan and Byzantine painting and all its decoration is carried out in full colour and gold. Especially striking is a series of initials, including figures, which introduce the Books of the Prophets.

Quite different in style is the great Bible from the Premonstratensian Abbey of Floreffe in Belgium, made about 1156 (Plate 19). It includes several outstanding full-page miniatures which betray a close relationship with Mosan metalwork of the same region, but most of its initials are in a subtle combination of black, brown and red penwork.

30

eneditus
dns ds ms
qui docet
manus me
as ad pre
lium. et
digitos
meos ao
bellum.
Misedia
mea et re

fugium meum: suseptoi ms & liberatoi ms.
Protectoi ms & inipso speraui: qui subdis popu
lum meum sub me.   quia reputas eu

If it has been correctly interpreted, the John the Baptist Roll (Plate 20) is a most unusual example of miniature painting. Now somewhat imperfect, it consists of nine consecutive scenes from the life of the saint painted upon two sides of a strip of vellum. It is thought that this may originally have been curved into a cylinder and provided with a handle for use as a liturgical fan or *flabellum*. The style of the miniatures, as far as can be judgéd, is closely related to that seen in a manuscript which was destroyed during the Franco-Prussian War of 1870, the *Hortus Deliciarum* of Herrad of Landsberg (1167–95). Both probably came from Alsace.

By the end of the twelfth century manuscript painting was moving stylistically from the Romanesque to the Gothic. A much softer type of modelling may be seen in the figures from a Psalter which seems to have been made for the Abbey of La-Charité-sur-Loire but which belonged to the nuns of Holy Cross at Poitiers by about 1200 (Plate 21). This manuscript originally had a decorated initial at the beginning of each psalm, usually containing a scene from the Old or New Testament. A great many of these are now missing, but enough remains to show the very high quality of the manuscript.

44

upales. Epanthenon. Egyptij. ū.
Oethm. Itali. Crocacim. Quidam ate
latirdem eam appellant. Vna
cura es. ad duritiem stomachi.
Herbam latirdis granum cum
popume purgatum fuit.
inaqua calida potatum dabis. sta
tim aluetum purgat. reum sanat.
Nomen huius herbe lactuca lepo
rina dr.

Dei aute meadem Item.ooo
herba umbilico infantium tri
ta rimposita pfectissime mede
ripsanat. Nomen istius herbe lati
rdis nuncupatur.

A grecis siquidem dr cocosmdos.
Quidamū camellam eam uocat.

Nascitur in locis cultis risablosis.
Lep autem inestate cum animo de
ficit. hanc herbam comedit. ideoq;
lactuca leporina dicat. Prima cu
ra ipsius. ad remediandum feb
erbam lactucam lectantem;

22. (*left*). HERBAL: *representations of medicinal plants.* England, about 1200. 95 folios. 295 × 200 mm. Sloane MS 1975, folio 44.

Although most of the finest early illumination is to be found in liturgical manuscripts, some secular texts were also commonly illustrated. Their number was to increase with increasing individual ownership of books. Medical science demanded a knowledge of herbs and many illuminated copies of the Greek Herbal of Pseudo-Apuleius, in Latin translation, have come down to us (Plate 22). The illustrations were originally intended to help the reader in identifying the plants, but copies made during this period, taken from earlier manuscripts rather than from living examples, reduced them to a stylized form very different from botanical reality. The text below each illustration gives first the characteristics of the plant and then its medicinal uses. Amongst additional materials included in this particular manuscript is a series of miniatures, without accompanying text, some depicting surgical operations and others charting the points on the body at which treatment by cauterization should be applied. Much of medieval medical science was a legacy from the classical world, but ideas were also received through contact with the Arabic settlers in Spain and southern Italy. As early as the tenth century Salerno, which is about thirty miles southeast of Naples, was famous for its physicians. The medical school which developed there was popularly supposed to have been founded by a Latin, a Greek, a Jew and a Saracen, these being the four main sources of medical knowledge.

23. BESTIARY: *the hyena.* England, about 1200. 112 folios. 225 × 160 mm. Royal MS 12 C. xix, folio 11b (detail).

Another 'scientific' work which usually includes illustrations is the Latin Bestiary, based upon the fifth-century *Physiologus*, heavily flavoured with Christian allegories and interpretations (Plate 23). Some of the animals and birds, including hedgehog, domestic cat, lion and elephant, are real and are given at least some recognizable attributes. Others, such as griffin and caladrius (a bird reputed to foretell the eventual fate of a sick man either by looking at him or by turning its head away), are fabulous. The creature identified in the Middle Ages as 'hyena' was said to live in tombs and to devour the flesh of the dead.

33

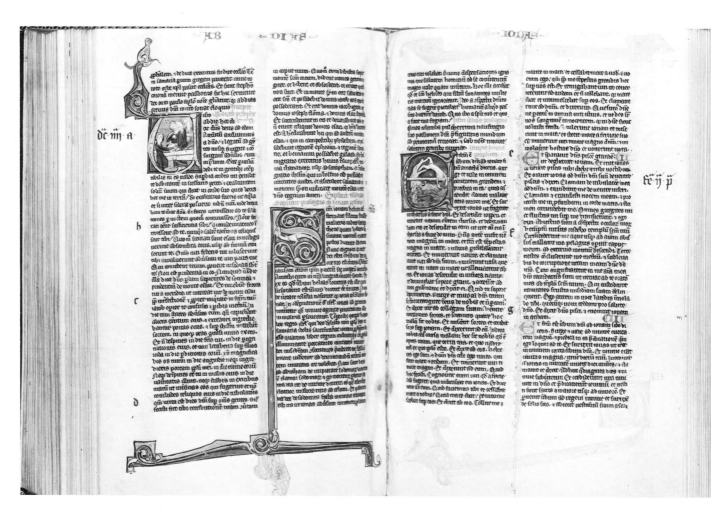

24. BIBLE: *initials to the books of the prophets Obadiah and Jonah.* France, early thirteenth century. 493 folios. 200 × 135 mm. Additional MS 27694, folios 334b-335.

25. BIBLE MORALISÉE: *Christ's miracles of healing.* France (Paris), about 1240. 153 folios. 395 × 275 mm. Harley MS 1527, folio 27.

At the beginning of the thirteenth century the rapid development of universities, together with the instant expansion of the new mendicant orders, the Franciscans and the Dominicans, both of which were specifically charged to travel and to teach, gave new impetus to commercial book production. This is especially reflected in an enormous number of pocket-sized Bibles, which often contain extensive series of tiny decorated initials (Plate 24). These little Bibles were valuable possessions, passed down from one owner to another, and it is quite common to find in them notes of the sums for which, in time of need, they were pawned to the university chest.

Another type of Bible characteristic of the thirteenth century is the *Bible moralisée*, every page of which looks very much like an elaborate design for a contemporary stained glass window. These were produced in Paris, largely under the patronage of the French royal family, and contain illustrations of incidents from the Old and New Testaments, in sequence, accompanied by parallel series of pictures representing their moral and allegorical interpretations. This page (Plate 25), chosen from a set of volumes containing more than six hundred in all, includes the miraculous raising of Jairus's daughter. Large numbers of illuminators worked on these books and the cost of producing them must have been immense.

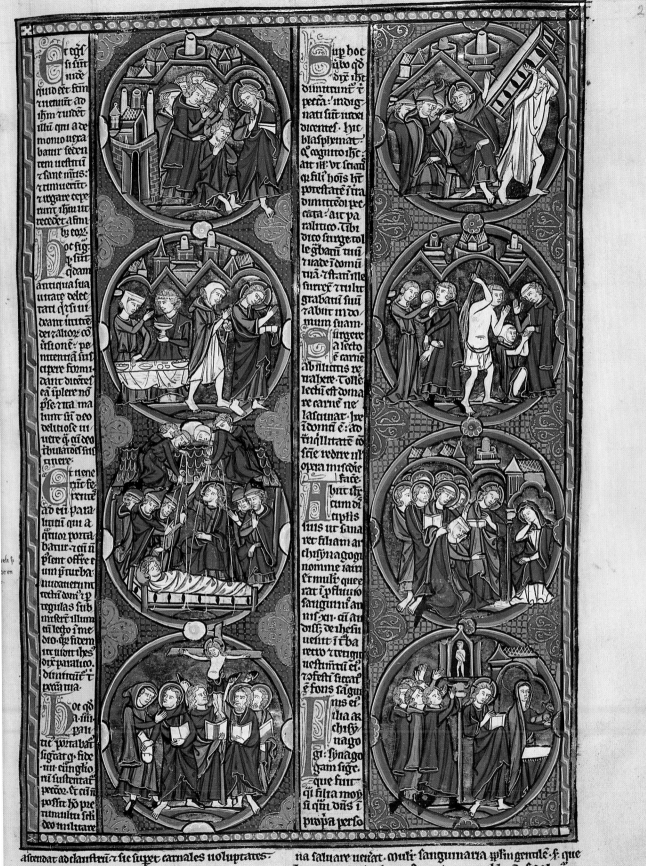

ascendat ad claustrū ⁊ sic supet carnales uoluptates.

na saluare ueniat mult sanguinaria ipsiu gentile. ⁊ que longo tempe ydolatrie fetore ⁊ carnis oblatōe fedabat

26. PSALTER: *Pentecost*. France (Paris), mid thirteenth century. 197 folios. 210 × 145 mm. Additional MS 17868, folio 29.

During the reign of St Louis (1126–70), himself a considerable patron, the professional illuminators of Paris were well supported, their work achieving a wide circulation. The Psalter from which the miniature of Pentecost (Plate 26) is drawn is one amongst many *de luxe* books which they made for anonymous private individuals. Contemporary records reveal that in cities such as Paris the various craftsmen involved in the production of books—illuminators, ink and parchment makers, bookbinders and so forth—tended to live side by side in specific streets or neighbourhoods, which made co-operation easy.

omme labia mea aperies;
et os meum annuntiabit

27. DE BRAILES HOURS: *the betrayal of Christ*. England (Oxford), mid thirteenth century. 105 folios.
150 × 120 mm. Additional MS 49999, folio 1.

This arrangement is traceable in Oxford, like Paris a university town, where book production was carried on in and around Catte Street. One of the illuminators named in Oxford records was W. de Brailes, and his signature appears in manuscripts of distinctive style made about the middle of the century. Amongst them is a Book of Hours, apparently the earliest to be made in England as a separate entity (Plate 27). The Hours had long been used as one of the adjuncts to the Psalter, but during the later Middle Ages it was rapidly to supersede it as the most usual book of private devotion. W. de Brailes seems to have painted all the decoration in this little manuscript personally, drawing his subjects from popular legends such as the Miracles of the Virgin as well as from the Bible.

28. PSALTER: *the Baptism of Christ*. Germany (Würzburg,) about 1240. 16 detached miniatures. 180 × 135 mm. Additional MS 17687 F.

29. EVESHAM PSALTER: *the Crucifixion*. England, after 1246. 284 folios. 315 × 210 mm. Additional MS 44874, folio 6.

Contemporary with the de Brailes Hours is a series of Psalter illustrations from Germany (Plate 28), painted in the Würzburg area, where a particularly flourishing school of illumination was active during the thirteenth century. These miniatures, which are of magnificent quality, are unfortunately no longer attached to a manuscript and the leaves which survive are divided between more than one collection. The jagged modelling of the draperies and a strong Byzantine influence are however characteristic of work produced in Germany at this period.

With the Evesham Psalter (Plate 29), also made about the middle of the thirteenth century, we reach another high-point in the history of English painting. Although this full-page miniature is the only one in the book, it is a masterpiece in which tinted drawing, full colour and gold are brilliantly combined. The kneeling figure at the foot of the page is an abbot of Evesham for whom the manuscript was made. The inclusion in the calendar of the feast of St Edmund Rich indicates a date after 1246. On one page the arms of Richard of Cornwall (d. 1272), brother of Henry III and brother-in-law of St Louis, have been added. Richard's interest in fine books was well known and it has been suggested that the Psalter may have been given to him as a peace-offering after the body of the rebellious Simon de Montfort, slain at the Battle of Evesham in 1265, had been buried in the abbey.

Five tinted drawings added in the mid-thirteenth century to a Psalter designed for Westminster use about 1200 are the work of a close associate of one of the leading artistic personalities of the time, Matthew Paris of St Albans (Plate 30). The wealthy Abbey of St Albans, conveniently situated one day's journey north of London, was used as a posting house by the high society of the period. Matthew Paris (d. 1259) was a monk there for forty-two years and became internationally known both for his chronicles and other writings and for his skills as a craftsman. He wrote out and illustrated many of his own books and all the characteristics of his style are reflected in the Westminster Psalter drawings. His friends included Henry III and such exalted members of the royal family as Richard of Cornwall and his wife Sanchia of Provence.

30. WESTMINSTER PSALTER: *St Christopher*. England (St Albans School), mid-thirteenth-century addition to a manuscript made about 1200. 224 folios. 225 × 160 mm. Royal MS 2 A. xxii, folio 220b.

40

31. APOCALYPSE: *the dragon bound and cast into the bottomless pit.* England (?St Albans), about 1260–70. 38 folios. 285 × 220 mm. Additional MS 35166, folio 26 (detail).

The Book of Revelation enjoyed a sudden and unexplained popularity as a picture book for both laymen and clerics in England, and to some extent in France, during the thirteenth century. The scriptorium at St Albans appears to have played a significant part in the production of copies. Tinted or coloured drawing, with a little gold, proved an excellent medium for lively illustrations of angels, monsters and dragons, inspired by the Apocalypse of St John (Plate 31).

English art, and especially English needlework, enjoyed a very high international reputation at this time. In 1965 a missing leaf from the Oscott Psalter was found, bearing on one side a miniature representing its original owner, and his identification underlines this point. He was Cardinal Ottobuone Fieschi, afterwards Pope Adrian V, who died in 1276. Immediately after the defeat of Simon de Montfort in 1265 he was appointed papal legate to England, where his main tasks were to make peace after the Barons' War and to preach the last crusade. He also enjoyed the personal friendship of Henry III and his family. His Psalter, an outstandingly beautiful manuscript, includes ten miniatures of individual saints (Plate 32) and nine pages of scenes from the life of Christ, but some picture pages are still missing.

The last crusade was a sequel to the fall of Antioch in 1268, Jerusalem having succumbed to the Saracens in 1244. It was led by St Louis, already a sick man, who died before he could reach the Holy Land. The only western stronghold then left in Palestine was Acre, which survived until 1291. During the thirteenth century Acre developed a fine manuscript tradition, largely concerned with the production of secular works of history and romance. This late *Histoire universelle* (Plate 33), in French, contains the finest work of a local artist, whose style combines Latin, Byzantine and even Arabic elements. He is known to have worked on occasion in collaboration with an illuminator who had migrated to Acre from France after an early period in Paris.

32. OSCOTT PSALTER: *St Peter*. England, about 1270. 257 folios. 300 × 190 mm. Additional MS 50000, folio 7b.

33. HISTOIRE UNIVERSELLE: *the Scythian women besieging their enemies*. Acre, about 1286. 314 folios. 370 × 250 mm. Additional MS 15268, folio 101b (detail).

Coment les dames de ſcite aleret
uengier loz barons ⁊ loz fiz ⁊ loz

lune roy ne ſepara quant elles fu
rent uengiez ⁊ lautre remeſt engꝛe.

Ntre elles auoit .ij. amis.
roynes: lune anomoit mer
peſia. ⁊ lautre lampeto. Juenes da
mes ⁊ belles de cors ⁊ de uiſages. ⁊
de cuer hardies. Ceſtes furent mlt
bien atoꝛner leur afaires. ſi come
poꝛ cheuauchier aforce ſur leur
annemis. ⁊ leur terres conquerre.
Mais anſois q̃lles iſſient ⁊ par
tiſſent de leur contrees: occiſtrent
elles tos les homes ⁊ les enfans

Nſi ⁊ par ceſte achaiſon co
menſierent pꝛemieꝛmēt
les dames en celle region apoꝛter
armes. q̃ puis deuindꝛent mlt
uaillanz ⁊ mlt cheualerouſes. ſi
come uos poꝛez aluos plaiſt a
uant oyr ⁊ entendre. Apꝛes ceſte
pꝛemeraine bataille q̃lles oꝛent
deſconfite ⁊ uencue: les .ij. roynes
merpſia ⁊ lampete: deuiſierent loꝛ
compaignie en .ij. parties. ⁊ ſire

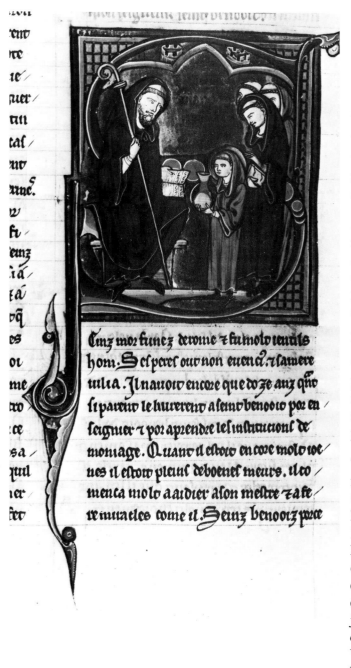

The *Histoire universelle* is an illustrated library book, probably designed for private reading. The collection of Legends of the Saints falls into the same class (Plate 34). It contains fifty-six saints' lives, translated into French from sundry Latin sources, and was probably made in northern France. The miniature reproduced comes from the life of St Maur, who became a disciple of St Benedict at the tender age of twelve. St Benedict, as the founder of western monasticism, had a profound influence on the life and thought of the Middle Ages.

Life in a religious community is portrayed in a miniature from *La Sainte Abbaye*, which ranks amongst the most delicate of all French thirteenth-century illumination (Plate 35). This copy was once part of a single volume in which *La Sainte Abbaye* appears with another religious treatise, *La Somme le Roy*, composed in 1279 for Philip III of France by the Dominican Père Laurent. This latter text, which deals with the Vices, is extremely boring by present-day standards, but it inspired a series of illustrations, known in several versions, which also reveal the very best in late thirteenth-century book painting.

The finest copy of *La Somme le Roy* (Plate 36) is a masterpiece of the outstanding personality in French Gothic painting, Maître Honoré, who is recorded as living and working in Paris between 1288 and about 1318. It is possible that he came from Amiens, which had a flourishing community of miniaturists, and his development was certainly influenced from north-eastern France and from England. Records and his existing manuscripts show that he worked in conjunction with other, less talented illuminators, one of whom is named as his son-in-law, Richard of Verdun. After Honoré's death Richard continued his work and in 1318 was paid for some manuscripts illuminated for the Sainte-Chapelle in Paris.

34. LEGENDS OF THE SAINTS: *St Maur and St Benedict.* Northern France, second half of the thirteenth century. 233 folios. 330 × 230 mm. Royal MS 20 D. vi, folio 200b (detail).

35. LA SAINTE ABBAYE: *the ideal nunnery.* France (Lorraine), late thirteenth century. 82 folios. 250 × 180 mm. Yates Thompson MS 11, folio 6b.

36. LA SOMME LE ROY: *Mercy and Avarice; Lot and the angels; the widow and her oil.* France (Paris), end of the thirteenth century. 208 folios. 185 × 120 mm. Additional MS 54180, folio 136b.

37. QUEEN MARY'S PSALTER: *the marriage at Cana.* England (?London), about 1310–20. 319 folios. 275 × 175 mm. Royal MS 2 B. vii, folio 168b.

The anonymous English artist who painted Queen Mary's Psalter (Plate 37) had a good deal in common with Honoré stylistically. The Psalter is of amazing richness, containing more than two hundred tinted drawings of Old Testament subjects and numerous fully-coloured miniatures from the New Testament, as well as small marginal scenes at the bottom of each of four hundred and sixty-four pages. The entire book is the work of a single artist, recognizable in several other books, who may possibly have been the head of a London workshop. There is no clue to the identity of the manuscript's first owner. It takes its name from Queen Mary Tudor, to whom it was presented in the sixteenth century by a customs officer who had prevented it from being taken out of the country.

46

aluum me fac ds:
qin intrauert aq
usq; ad atam mea.
n fixus sum i li

38. BOOK OF HOURS: *the three living and the three dead.* Holland (Maastricht), about 1300. 273 folios. 95 × 70 mm. Stowe MS 17, folios 199b–200.

Marginal scenes are a particular characteristic of early fourteenth-century books from both sides of the Channel. Subjects might be religious or secular and popular stories very often appear, divided into episodes over a number of pages. The small-scale Psalters and Books of Hours produced in the Low Countries at this period are a rich source of such scenes. In the Hours from the Stowe collection one opening shows the well-known encounter between three living kings and three desiccated corpses who warn them: 'As we are now, so shall you be' (Plate 38).

Although illuminated books were an expensive luxury, it would be a mistake to suppose that all the most elaborate ones were made exclusively for royalty or for the higher ranks of the nobility. In England particularly the reverse is often true. The great Psalters of the East Anglian School were in several cases commissioned by people who, although well-to-do landowners, were certainly not among the greatest in the land. The intricate St Omer Psalter (Plate 39), made about 1330, was intended for an otherwise unmemorable family of that name living at Mulbarton in Norfolk. The original owner and his wife are included amongst the decoration at the foot of the page.

39. ST OMER PSALTER: *'Beatus' page.* England (East Anglia), about 1330. 175 folios. 335 × 225 mm. Yates Thompson MS 14, folio 7.

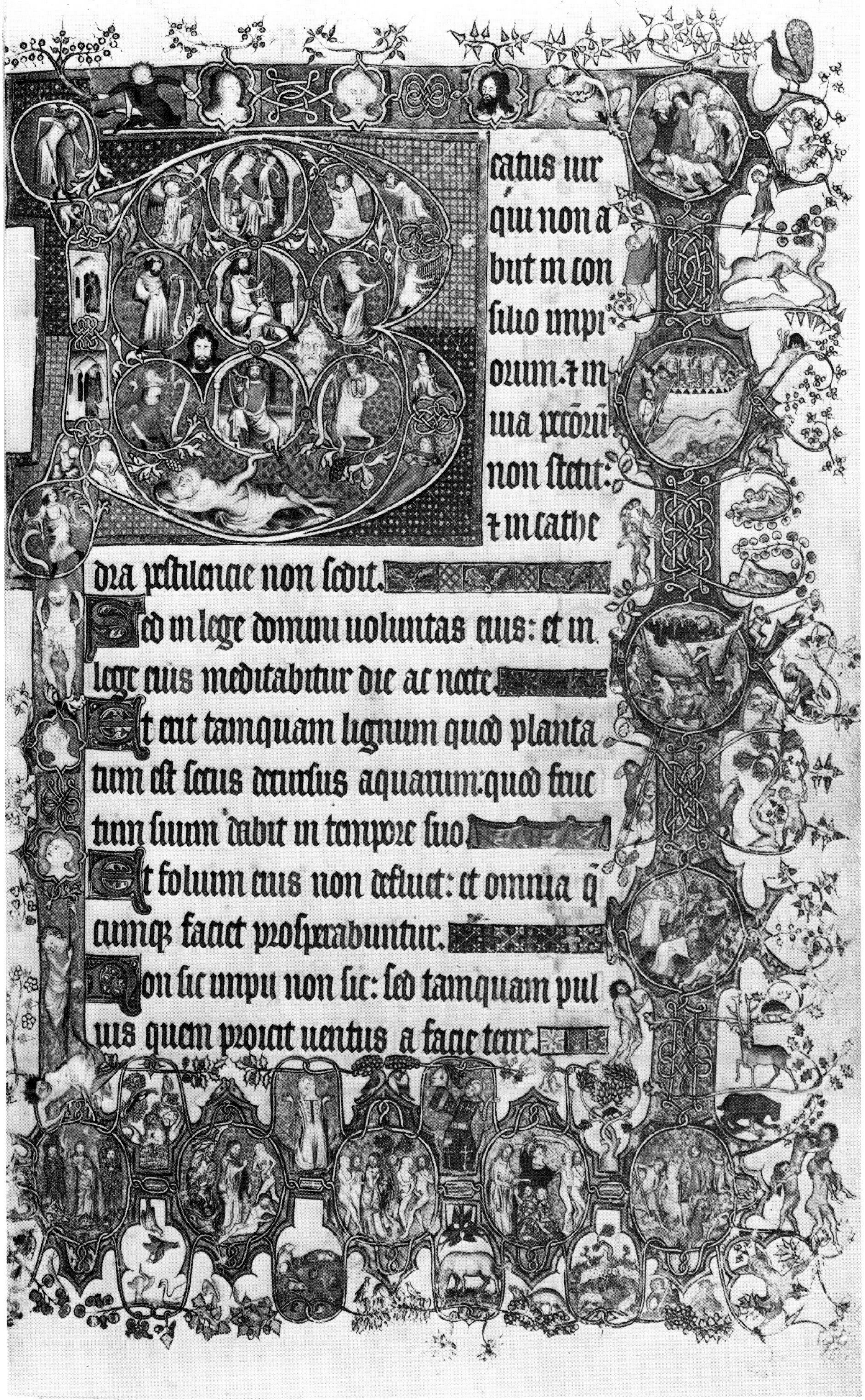

eatus uir
qui non a
biit in con
silio impi
orum. ⁊ in
uia pctorū
non stetit:
⁊ in cathe
dia pstilencie non sedit.

Sed in lege dominu uoluntas eius: et in
lege eius meditabitur die ac nocte.

Et erit tamquam lignum quod planta
tum est secus decursus aquarum:quod fruc
tum suum dabit in tempore suo.

Et folium eius non defluet: et omnia q
cumque faciet prosperabuntur.

Non sic impii non sic: sed tamquam pul
uis quem proicit uentus a facie terre.

omnes qui confidunt in eis
Domus israel sperauit in domino:
adiutor eorum + protector eorum est.
Domus aaron sperauit in domino:
adiutor eorum + protector eorum est.
Qui timent dominum sperauerunt

40. LUTTRELL PSALTER: *kitchen scene*. England, about 1335–40. 309 folios. 350 × 245 mm. Additional MS 42130, folio 207 (detail).

41. HAGGADAH: *Israel in Egypt*. Spain, fourteenth century. 161 folios. 250 × 185 mm. Additional MS 14761, folio 30b.

One patron particularly remembered for the manuscript which bears his name is Sir Geoffrey Luttrell of Irnham in Lincolnshire (d. 1345). The marginal decorations in his Psalter include scenes of everyday life, both indoors and out, which have provided the illustrations for countless popular history books (Plate 40). One marginal sequence follows each stage in the annual cultivation of the crops. Another shows the kitchens hard at work before a banquet. Sir Geoffrey's cook, John of Bridgford, is mentioned by name in his will and the bald and bearded figure at the cauldrons may represent him. The style of the Luttrell Psalter is less polished than that found in the Queen Mary or St Omer manuscripts, but it surpasses them in vitality.

The majority of Gothic manuscripts provide some reflections of contemporary life, because the idea of representing even biblical scenes in any but the idiom of their own times was quite alien to medieval artists. Contemporary building methods are thus used by Israelites building a city for the Egyptians in a Passover Haggadah made in Spain in the fourteenth century (Plate 41). During the Middle Ages large Jewish communities were settled throughout Europe. The Haggadah was used domestically by individual families and luxury copies were privately commissioned just as Psalters and Hours were commissioned by Christian families. We do not know whether Jewish manuscripts were usually made by Jewish artists to order in Christian workshops, but they were certainly made in the styles locally current in their countries of adoption.

50

42. ADDRESS OF THE CITY OF PRATO TO ROBERT OF ANJOU:
the judgement of Paris. Italy (Tuscany), 1335–40.
30 folios. 480 × 340 mm. Royal MS 6 E. ix, folio 22.

43. COMPENDIUM OF MEDICINAL PLANTS: *picking cherries*.
Northern Italy, second half of the fourteenth century.
108 folios. 365 × 260 mm. Sloane MS 4016, folio 30.

Cerasia. sap. aut
ceresia.

cera citrina.

Cepe domestice.
arabice. basal.
ul'abbasale uel
adlusal.

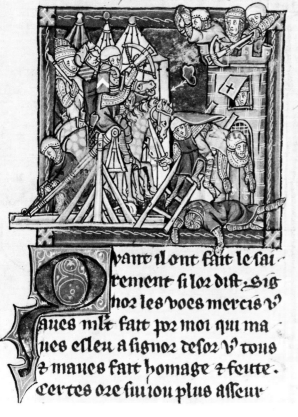

By the beginning of the fourteenth century the work of Italian painters on panel was influencing painters north of the Alps. The spread of this influence was assisted by close links between Italy and France through the exiled papal court at Avignon after 1309 and through the Angevin rulers of Naples. The miniatures in the address from the Tuscan town of Prato to Robert of Anjou are themselves almost large enough to rank with panel paintings (Plate 42). Robert, King of Naples and Count of Provence 1309–43, was the friend and patron of Giotto.

A new awareness of nature in Italian painting was also to have a profound effect on European illumination. A number of scientific works illustrated in northern Italy during the second half of the fourteenth century include botanical subjects apparently drawn from life (Plate 43). Marriage alliances between successive generations of the ducal house of Milan and the royal family of France provided a link to help the spread of this development.

Large illustrated volumes of history and romance, suitable for entertainment rather than for instruction, became increasingly popular everywhere during the thirteenth and fourteenth centuries. Their usual language is French, which was almost universally used by the educated upper class to which they appealed. Amongst their principal heroes are Alexander the Great, Charlemagne and, in a large number of stories which include the *Roman du Saint Graal* (Plate 44), King Arthur and his knights. These characters, like the biblical ones, are portrayed in contemporary settings and supplied with the latest models in armour and siege equipment.

44. ROMAN DU SAINT GRAAL: *Mordred besieging the Tower of London.* Flanders, early fourteenth century. 96 folios. 405 × 295 mm. Additional MS 10294, folio 81b (detail).

45. FAITS DES ROMAINS: *a storm at sea.* Italy (Naples), about 1340. 363 folios. 330 × 230 mm. Royal
MS 20 D. i, folio 176b (detail).

The *Faits des Romains*, drawn from a variety of sources, covers ancient history from Thebes in the time of Œdipus to Rome in the time of Pompey. It includes tales of Alexander the Great and also those of the Siege of Troy. Made in Naples towards the end of the reign of Robert of Anjou, this copy follows the Italian fashion of having its miniatures in the lower margins (Plate 45). Its artists seem to have enjoyed attempting to capture the appearance of natural phenomena. In this miniature Greek ships leaving conquered Troy are caught in a violent storm, with hailstones lashing a heaving sea.

55

Acapit colonam regni. in nomine pa

46. CORONATION BOOK OF CHARLES V: *peers supporting the crown*. France (Paris), 1365. 108 folios. 280 × 190 mm. Cotton MS Tiberius B. viii, folio 59b (detail).

47. BIBLE HISTORIALE, VOL. I: *the Holy Trinity*. France (Paris), 1357. 264 folios. 395 × 295 mm. Royal MS 17 E. vii, folio 1.

One of the earliest serious collectors of a large secular library was Charles V of France, who succeeded to the throne in 1364 when his father, John the Good, who had been captured by the English at the Battle of Poitiers in 1356, died after spending most of the rest of his life as a prisoner in England. Charles V commissioned a fully-illustrated record of his own coronation (Plate 46) and is recognizably portrayed in a number of its thirty-eight miniatures. He is amongst the earliest historical figures whose true appearance was captured for the future. By the time of his death his library was to contain about nine hundred manuscripts.

John the Good had been a patron of the arts and his other sons, Louis Duke of Anjou (d. 1384), Philip Duke of Burgundy (d. 1404) and John Duke of Berry (d. 1416), all became noted book collectors. The copy of Guyart des Moulins's *Bible historiale* provides a very good example of the best French illumination of the mid fourteenth century (Plate 47). It was made in the year after Poitiers, in fashionable and restrained semi-grisaille heightened with patches of colour and with gold, and is attributed to the Maître aux Boquetaux, so named because of his habit of including groups of little rounded bushes in his compositions.

56

Ci commence la Bible
hystoriaus. ou les hystoires
escolastres. Cest li prologues
de celui qui mist ce liure de la
tin en francois

ontre que
li dyables
qui chascun
iour en pe
chie destour
be et enord
dist les cu
ers des hommes par oyseuse
et par mil las quil a tendu

pour nous prendre. et en
trer en nos cuers. Com cil
qui onques ne cesse de gue
tier comment il nous puisse
mieuer a pechie pour nos ame
ner en son puant cuiter.
auecques lui. Est il mestier
a nous clers et prestres de
sainte eglise. qui deuons es
tre lumier du monde. que
nous apz nos liures z nos
oroisons entendons a aucu
ne bonne cuiter fair. si que
li pers des dampnes. Ant

il nous vient assaillir ne
nous truisse oyseus par qy
il ait achoison de legiermet
entrer en nos cuers. Et nous
face cheoir par pense. Pre
mierement par pense. Et
apres par euure. Si deuons
sur toute riens fur oyseuse
Et entendre touziours a fai
re aucune bonne euure qui
a dieu plaise. et au dyable
soit contraire et ennuieuse
Et pource que li dyables qui
maintes foiz ma fait pechier

The use of grisaille was not confined to French illuminators. It is employed in a series of illustrations for the fictitious *Travels* of Sir John Mandeville, made in Austria during the early years of the fifteenth century (Plate 48). In this manuscript the surface of each page is tinted a delicate shade of green. Only the hands and faces of the figures, the trees and a dark-blue sky spangled with golden stars add further colour to the miniature. The *Travels* was composed about 1356 in the Low Countries and was translated into many languages. Based on a variety of earlier sources, it was probably originally intended only to serve as a guide for pilgrims visiting the Holy Land, but it was expanded to cover legends of the unknown lands further east. It enjoyed enormous popularity and survives in about three hundred manuscripts, far more than the factual account of Marco Polo's journey to China in the late thirteenth century.

Although the emphasis during the late Middle Ages was upon the provision of books for private patrons, many manuscripts were also made for public use. Such are the volumes of liturgical music which were made from the late thirteenth century onwards, particularly in Italy. Often lavishly decorated, they were designed on a very large scale, to be placed on lecterns from which they could be visible to a whole group of singers at once. This example was made for the Augustinian hermits of San Salvatore in Siena (Plate 49). Books of this type continued to be made and used until comparatively recent times.

48. SIR JOHN MANDEVILLE'S TRAVELS: *the philosophers on Mount Athos*. Austria, early fifteenth century. 16 folios. 225 × 180 mm. Additional MS 24189, folio 15.

49. HYMNAL: *the Resurrection*. Italy (Siena), 1415. 213 folios. 395 × 275 mm. Additional MS 30014, folio 80b.

Agni moundi . et stolis

albis candidi . post tren

50. BIBLIA PAUPERUM: *the Resurrection, paralleled by Samson breaking down the gates and Jonah escaping from the whale.* Holland, beginning of the fifteenth century. 31 folios. 175 × 380 mm. Kings MS 5, folio 20.

51. BREVIARY OF JOHN THE FEARLESS: *the Ascension.* France (Paris), about 1415. 453 folios. 250 × 180 mm. Harley MS 2897, folio 188b.

The term International Gothic is applied to the arts in the early fifteenth century because there was so general an exchange of influences throughout Europe. One of the strongest infusions came from Dutch painters such as those who were responsible for the miniatures in the *Biblia pauperum* (Plate 50). The original text for this work came from Germany but it found especial favour in the contemporary devotional climate of Holland. The miniatures are very simple in composition and have a touching human flavour, but their quality is superb.

The Limbourg brothers, possibly the most celebrated miniaturists of all time, protégés of the Duke of Berry and the illuminators of his *Très Riches Heures* (now in the Musée Condé at Chantilly), were Dutch by birth. A Breviary produced in their circle for Berry's nephew, John the Fearless, Duke of Burgundy (assassinated in 1419), affords a magnificent example of the style which is associated with them (Plate 51). The arms of the Duke and of his wife, Margaret of Bavaria, are held by the seated figure of a lady in the margin below the miniature.

The English victory at Agincourt in 1415 was followed in 1420 by a treaty providing for the crowns of France and England to be united. When Henry V, victor of Agincourt, died in 1422, leaving an infant heir, it fell to his brother John, Duke of Bedford, to act for him in France. In 1423 Bedford cemented the English alliance with Burgundy by marrying Anne, sister of the reigning Duke Philip the Good. Their marriage, which was contracted for political reasons but which turned into a love match, is commemorated in the Bedford Hours, which includes miniatures of the duke and duchess with their patron saints (Plate 52). The book was ordered from a leading Parisian workshop, whose chief illuminator is nowadays identified as the Bedford Master.

Bedford also owned a magnificent Psalter and Hours illuminated in England in the workshop of Herman Scheerre (Plate 53). Scheerre probably came from the Lower Rhineland and he and his associates were a major influence in the style which emerged in England at this time. Dutch influence was also strongly felt and many manuscripts for English patrons were in fact imported from the Low Countries. Especially noteworthy in the Bedford Psalter are dozens of tiny but intensely lifelike portrait faces filling the minor initials on every page.

60

52. BEDFORD HOURS: *the Duchess of Bedford with her patron, St Anne.* France (Paris), about 1423. 289 folios. 260 × 180 mm. Additional MS 18850, folio 257b.

53. BEDFORD PSALTER AND HOURS: *the Tree of Jesse; Samuel anointing David.* England (London), about 1420. 240 folios. 405 × 280 mm. Additional MS 42131, folio 73.

Eatus uir qui
non abijt i con
silio impioru:
et in uia pecca
torum non ste
tit. et in cathed
pestilencie non
sedit. Sed in
lege domini uoluntas eius: et in lege ei'
meditabitur die ac nocte. Et erit tan
qm lignum quod plantatum est secus
decursus aquarum: quod fructu suum
dabit in tempore suo Et folium eius
non defluet: et omnia quecunqz faciet
prosperabuntur Non sic impij non
sic: sed tanquam puluis quem proicit
uentus a facie terre Ideo non resur
gunt impij in iudicio: neqz pecdores in

La magior ualle in che lacqua sispanda
in cominciaro allor le sue parole
suor diquella mar che la terra igherlanda

Tra discordanti liti contra sole
tanto sen ua che fa meridiano
la doue lorizonte pia far sole

Diquella ualle suio litorano
tra ebro et magra che pciamin corto
parte lo genouese dal toscano

55. DANTE'S *Divina Commedia: the corruption of the Florentines* (*Paradiso IX*, 127–32). Italy (Siena), about 1440. 190 folios. 365 × 260 mm. Yates Thompson MS 36, folio 145 (detail).

Italian scholars of the early fifteenth century were renowned for their rediscovery and study of the ancient classics. Copies of new-found texts in Latin and Greek and in vernacular translations were eagerly sought after and were circulated in beautifully written and decorated copies. Aristotle's *Ethics* is in the tradition of these books, though it was in fact written and illuminated in Spain (Plate 54). It was translated into Spanish by Charles, Prince of Viana (d. 1461), for his uncle Alfonso V of Aragon, King of Naples, shortly after whose death in 1458 this copy was made.

54. ARISTOTLE'S *Ethics*, IN SPANISH: *opening page*. Spain, 1458–61. 238 folios. 320 × 225 mm. Additional MS 21120, folio 1.

Alfonso V and his successors at Naples created another celebrated royal library and to this the Yates Thompson Dante at one time belonged (Plate 55). The *Divina Commedia* had attracted an extensive cycle of illustrations within a short time of its author's death in 1321. Numerous copies are known, of which this is amongst the most beautiful. With its one hundred and fifteen miniatures it may certainly claim to be the finest secular manuscript produced in fifteenth-century Siena. The *Paradiso* illustrations are attributed to Giovanni di Paolo (d. about 1482), who is also celebrated for his panel paintings. This illustration shows the evil done by the Florentine golden florin, on which the lily emblem of the city is stamped. Dante illustrations

65

56. LYDGATE'S *Life of St Edmund: King Lothbrok going hunting*. England, after 1433. 119 folios. 250 × 170 mm. Harley MS 2278, folio 41b (detail).

are peculiar to Italy because his great work, written in vernacular poetry rather than in vernacular prose, did not lend itself to direct translation into other languages.

The most famous of English medieval vernacular poems is the *Canterbury Tales* of Geoffrey Chaucer (d. 1400), but, although this survives in some eighty copies, only the well-known Ellesmere Chaucer (now in the Huntington Library in California) includes any noteworthy illustrations. The works of John Lydgate (d. about 1450), court poet to Henry V and his son Henry VI, were, however, quite frequently illuminated. Outstanding among them is a copy of his *Life of St Edmund* (Plate 56), made at the order of the abbot of Bury St Edmunds as a gift for twelve-year-old Henry VI, after he had spent Christmas with the monks in 1433. No exact parallel has yet been suggested for the style of its miniatures, but the artist showed a particular talent for endowing with personalities the many animals included in the story.

57. SPIEGEL DER WEISHEIT: *the fox and the raven*. Austria, first quarter of the fifteenth century. 127 folios. 260 × 190 mm. Egerton MS 1121, folio 7b (detail).

Lively and individual animals also inhabit the miniatures of the *Spiegel der Weisheit*, a German version of a collection of Latin fables (Plate 57). It was translated about 1415 by an Austrian priest, Ulrich von Pottenstein, who was at one time chaplain to the Austrian Duke Albrecht IV. This copy reflects the style of the Austrian court school of the early fifteenth century.

58. BIBLE IN DUTCH: *Samuel's father, Elkanah the Levite, with his two wives, Penninah and Hannah.* Holland, about 1440. 301 folios. 385 × 285 mm. Additional MS 15410, folio 177b (detail).

59.(*opposite*). VALERIUS MAXIMUS' *Memorabilia,* PART I: *Octavian's court; the siege of Capua.* France (Paris), about 1475. 253 folios. 475 × 350 mm. Harley MS 4374, folio 88.

In Holland the major personality amongst illuminators of the second quarter of the fifteenth century was the Master of Catherine of Cleves, named from an Hours which he painted about 1440 for Catherine Duchess of Guelders (now in the Pierpont Morgan Library, New York). His hand also occurs in several Dutch vernacular Bibles of about the same date and he is particularly noted for some illustrations carried out in line drawing. His fully-coloured work (Plate 58) is itself somewhat linear in feeling, especially by comparison with that of his earlier compatriot, the artist of the *Biblia pauperum.*

Particularly characteristic of the late fifteenth century, especially in France and in the Low Countries, are very large and sumptuous library copies of historical and literary works. Some of these are executed on a scale comparable with that of the great Bibles of the Romanesque period. The French translation of the *Memorabilia* of the Roman writer Valerius Maximus was popular, and the copy of it made about 1475 for the French historian Philippe de Commines is a fine example of this type of book (Plate 59). The owner's arms appear at the top of the miniature and his initial, entwined with that of his wife Hélène, occurs twice within the left-hand side of the composition. The manuscript was produced in the Parisian workshop of an illuminator called Maître François, one of the most prolific book painters of the time.

One of the most exciting manuscript discoveries of recent years has been the Hastings Hours (Plate 60), bequeathed to the nation by Mrs C. W. Dyson Perrins, who died in 1968. This manuscript was made about 1480 for William Lord Hastings, a close friend of Edward IV. Hastings was beheaded in 1483 on the orders of the Duke of Gloucester, afterwards Richard III. Its delicate and beautiful miniatures and decoration place it among the very finest of the manuscripts produced in Flanders by the founders of the Ghent/Bruges School, one of the last great styles of illumination. Hastings's arms, surrounded by the Garter, appear in the margin of the page opposite the Annunciation.

uices et preuotes pour lors estoient. Maintenant
Apres ce q en ce second liure et es autres li
halerius ures ensuiuans Il parle et met
a parle ou pmier exemples des choses qui peuent
liure des choses mouuoir a bonnes meurs. Et
qui appartiennent au seruice premierement Il met son prolos
et honneur des dieux selon les me en continuant ce second liu
romains et les autres grs qui a la fin du pmier et dit ainsi

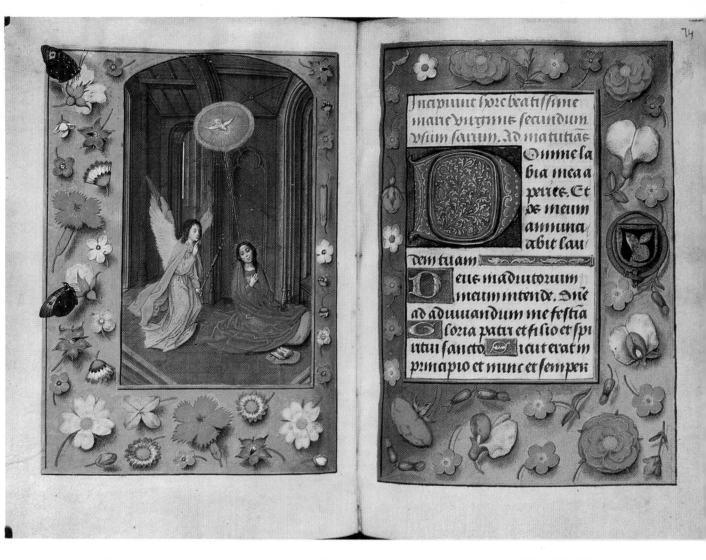

60. HASTINGS HOURS: *the Annunciation*. Flanders (Bruges or Ghent), about 1480. 297 folios. 165 × 120 mm. Additional MS 54872, folios 73b–74.

For some months in 1470–1 Edward IV, attended by his brother-in-law Lord Rivers and by Hastings, was in exile in Flanders, entertained in Bruges by Louis de Gruthuyse, one of the great bibliophiles of the age. Louis's example inspired Edward to order from Bruges, probably through his sister Margaret, who was married to the Duke of Burgundy, large numbers of illuminated library copies of literary and historical works, thus laying the foundations of the English royal library. The Boccaccio, its border decoration incorporating Edward's arms and badges, is one of these (Plate 61). Its text is a French translation from the Italian made in 1409 for the Duke of Berry by Laurent de Premierfait. The dedication miniature, which purports to show the translation being presented to its original patron, provides a detailed study of a reception room in Edward's own time. Edward's bibliographical interests were not to be confined to manuscripts. He, his sister, and both his companions in exile were all amongst the patrons of William Caxton, who introduced printing into England from Flanders in 1476.

61. BOCCACCIO'S *Des cas des nobles hommes et femmes malheureux: Laurent de Premierfait presenting his translation to John, Duke of Berry*. Flanders (Bruges), about 1480. 513 folios. 480 × 335 mm. Royal MS 14 E. v, folio 5.

70

Puissant noble
et excellent prince
Jehan filz du Roy
de france Duc de
berry et dauuer
gne. Conte de poitou. destampes. de
bousongne. et dauuergne. Ian
rens de premier fait Clerc et dostre
moms digne secretaire et serf de
bonne soy toute obeissance et subgec
tion due. comme a mon tresredoub
te seigneur et bienfaiteur et act

thrablement Receuoir se sabeur de
mon estude et benignement execu
ser la petitece de mon engin au re
gard de la grunt besongne de dre
commandement ja piece entrepri
se et nouuellement finee. Combien
que pur dostre especial mandement
Jare soubz la consiance de dostre
naturele benignite et en espoir de
dostre gracieux ayde et confort. en
treprins se langeraux et song tin
ueil de la translation dui treseur

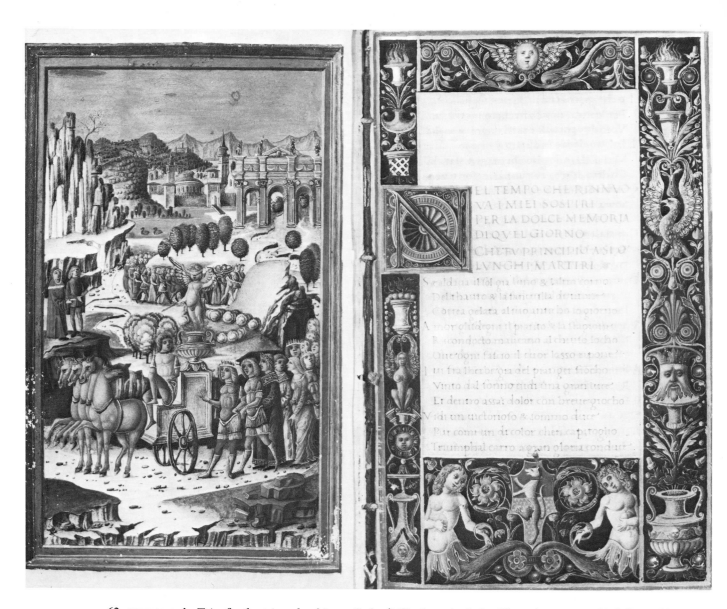

62. PETRARCH'S *Trionfi: the triumph of Love.* Italy (Milan), end of the fifteenth century. 88 folios. 200 ×
125 mm. Additional MS 38125, folios 33b–34.

Illuminated books made in Italy at the end of the
fifteenth century, although certainly as richly
decorated, almost never approach the vast scale of
those made north of the Alps. The *Trionfi* of Petrarch
(d. 1374) represents the best Lombard work of the
period (Plate 62). It was made for the Romei family
of Ferrara and is related to the paintings of Giovan
Pietro Birago, who worked for the Sforza Dukes of
Milan. Petrarch's vernacular poetry, like that of
Dante, inspired mainly Italian illuminators and the
Trionfi were frequently illustrated.

Henry VII of England, who defeated the last
Yorkist king, Richard III, at Bosworth in 1485,

continued to build up the royal library which
Edward IV had begun. His first named librarian was
Quintin Poulet from Lille and he presented his
master in 1496 with this copy of *Imaginacion de
vraye noblesse*, a discourse on nobility composed in
Hainault about half a century earlier (Plate 63).
The manuscript is typically Flemish in style and
includes the illusionistic borders, filled with
naturalistic flowers, which were one of the hallmarks
of the Ghent/Bruges School.

63. IMAGINACION DE VRAYE NOBLESSE: *shooting at the
butts.* England (Richmond Palace), 1496. 47 folios.
310 × 215 mm. Royal MS 19 C. viii, folio 41.

Plus que iay parle de lestat de che
ualerie ie vueil monstrer par
evamples auv roys auv prinas
et seigneurs qui leur est de neces
site plus que autres personnes
dauoir sens z entendement car presuppose quilz
ayent des leurs ieunesse estez bien instruiz/ou quilz

64. BOOK OF HOURS: *floral decorations*. France (Paris), 1515–20. 141 folios. 130 × 90 mm.
Additional MS 35214, folios 49b–50.

Where Flemish artists usually chose to portray either single flower heads or small sprays in their borders, French artists were more inclined to paint whole plants. In the Hours of Anne of Brittany (now in the Bibliothèque Nationale in Paris), made about 1508 for the queen of Louis XII and attributed to the court painter Jean Bourdichon of Tours, the margins of the text pages contain more than three hundred plants, each one identified by both its Latin and its French name. Of exceptional delicacy are the flower and plant paintings in a tiny Book of Hours made about a decade later, which belongs to a group of miniature prayer-books including manuscripts made for Anne's daughter Claude, wife of Louis's successor, Francis I (Plate 64).

To Bourdichon himself may be attributed the detached miniature of the Virgin receiving the Annunciation (Plate 65), part of a fine manuscript from which nine miniatures and fifty-three leaves of text have so far been recognized. The text leaves have long been traditionally associated with Henry VII and there is certainly no reason why he should not have owned the book. Bourdichon treated his miniatures as small-scale paintings and usually defined them within a gold frame. He seems to have been fascinated by direct and visible sources of light, here represented by the rays from the Holy Dove falling upon the Virgin's face.

65. HOURS OF HENRY VII: *the Virgin receiving the Annunciation*. France (Tours), about 1500. Detached leaf. 240 × 170 mm. Additional MS 35254 V.

66. TREATISE ON FALCONRY by Giovanni Pietro Balbasso of Vigevano: *a hawking party*. France (Paris), 1510–31. 278 folios. 300 × 200 mm. Additional MS 25092, folios 11b–12.

Bourdichon died in 1521, shortly after working on pavilion decorations for the meeting of Francis I and Henry VIII at the Field of the Cloth of Gold. In clear contrast to his somewhat placid style is the work of a contemporary group of French miniaturists obviously influenced by the technique of the engraver. One of them was responsible for the lively frontispiece to Giovanni Pietro Balbasso's treatise on falconry (Plate 66), the text of which is dated 1510 and which bears the arms of Guillaume de Montmorency (d. 1531), chamberlain to Charles VIII, Louis XII and Francis I. Miniatures in this style were still being produced in the 1540s and have been recognized in printed as well as in manuscript books.

In Flanders the second generation of the Ghent/ Bruges School, prominent among whom was Simon Bening (d. 1561), continued to make sumptuous Books of Hours. Bening himself may have painted the miniatures in the Hours made about 1516 for seventeen-year-old Joanna of Ghistelles, nominated abbess of Messines, near Ypres, in that year by the Emperor Charles V. The manuscript (Plate 67) includes the ceremonies of Vesture and Unction for the use of an abbess of Messines, and the patrons of the community, including its eleventh-century foundress, Countess Adela of Flanders, are prominent in its calendar. Joanna's connection with the book is suggested by the presence of a rhymed office for St Godelieva, the wife of Bertulph of Ghistelles, who was strangled by servants acting on the orders of her husband in 1070. Godelieva was quickly recognized as a saint and thereafter regarded as the martyr-patron of her husband's home. Simon Bening was born about 1483 in Ghent, where his father Alexander was already a well-known illuminator. For most of his long career he was established in Bruges, and so many elaborate manuscripts are attributed to his hand that we must assume he had a substantial atelier there. The illusionistic floral borders which are such a feature of the Hastings Hours (Plate 60) were frequently used by him, but more usually as an accessory to pages of text than in conjunction with miniatures. Here, like Bourdichon, he uses only a simple gold frame as a border, creating the impression of a small panel painting.

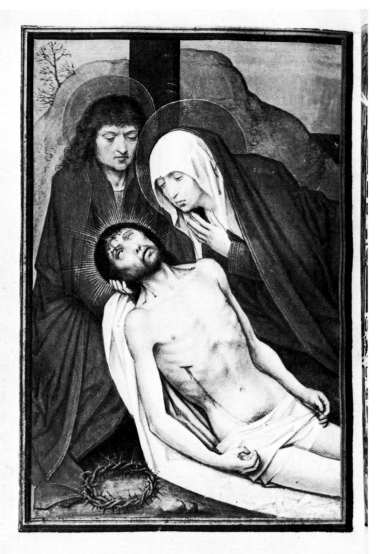

67. HOURS OF JOANNA OF GHISTELLES: *Pietà*. Flanders (Bruges), about 1516. 220 folios. 150 × 105 mm. Egerton MS 2125, folio 154b.

68. TRIUMPHS OF THE EMPEROR CHARLES V: *the raising of the siege of Vienna, 1529*. Italy (Rome), about 1556. 18 folios. 200 × 285 mm. Additional MS 33733, folio 9.

The victories of Charles V, who abdicated several years before his death in 1558, are recorded in a sequence of twelve colourful miniatures accompanied by short verses in Spanish (Plate 68). These illustrations are in the elaborate style evolved by Giulio Clovio, the most celebrated miniaturist in Italy in the mid sixteenth century. Clovio was born in Croatia in 1498, but moved to Italy as a young man and there received much encouragement from Giulio Romano, a pupil of Raphael. The works of Michelangelo, whom he much admired, are also reflected in his miniatures. The illuminated Triumphs of Charles V are paralleled in a series of engravings and may not be by Clovio's own hand but by that of a close follower. They were apparently made for Charles's son, King Philip II of Spain.

Also designed for Philip II is the atlas by the Portuguese map-maker, Diogo Homem, produced about 1558 (Plate 69). On the map of Europe Philip's arms are associated with those of his wife, Mary I of England, who died in November of that year. Both Portugal and Spain had been very active in the exploration and settlement of the Americas during the decades which followed Columbus's pioneering voyage in 1492. In the atlas Homem, a member of a well-known family of cartographers, uses the traditional techniques of the medieval illuminator to illustrate the native inhabitants and customs of the New World.

69. ATLAS BY DIOGO HOMEM: *South America*. Portugal, about 1558. 24 folios. 580 × 410 mm. Additional MS 5415 A, folios 23b–24.

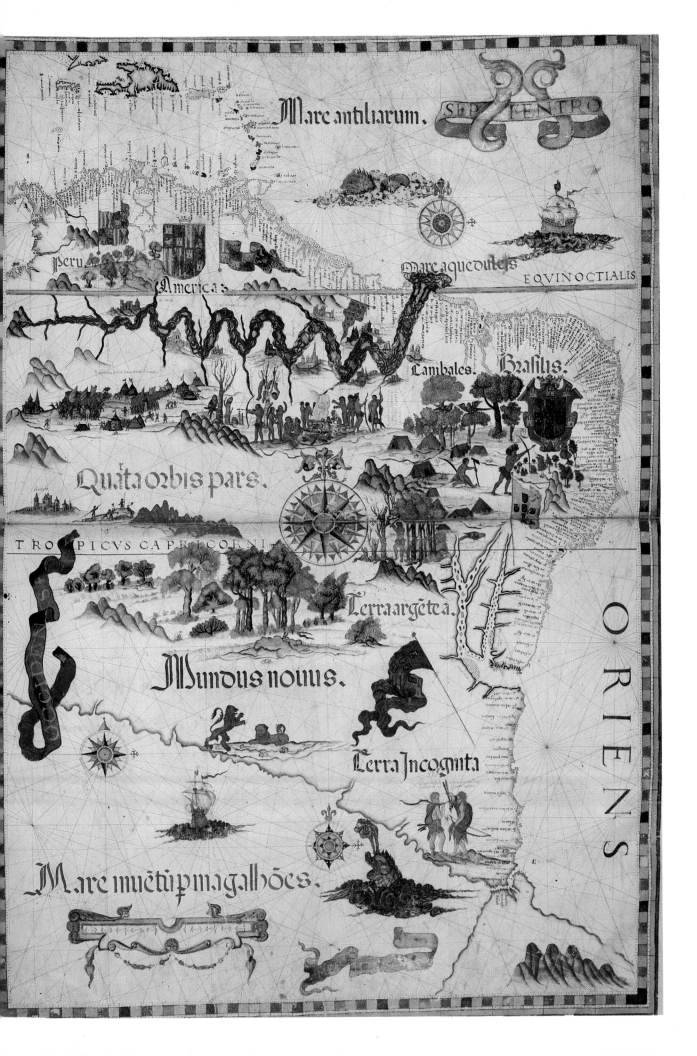

Mare antiliarum.

SEPTENTRIO

Peru

America

Mare aquedulcis

EQVINOCTIALIS

Canibales.

Brasilis.

Quãta orbis pars.

TROPICVS CAPRICORNI

Terra argẽtea.

Mundus nouus.

Terra Incognita

O R I E N S

Mare muetupmagalhões.

70. BOETHIUS' *De consolatione philosophiae: dedication page*. Printed in Paris by Antoine Vérard, 1494, and illuminated. 143 folios. 345 × 240 mm. C. 22. f. 8, folio 2.

Clovio and Homem produced their manuscripts at a time when the printed book had already usurped most of the market supplied in earlier centuries by the scribes and illuminators. Printing had been introduced throughout Europe by the time Columbus set sail for the Americas. Some printers, including the leading Parisian publisher Antoine Vérard, who established his business in 1485, produced for their more exalted clients books which, printed on vellum and illuminated by hand, closely resemble manuscripts. A Boethius from the English royal library provides a fine example of this kind of book (Plate 70). Its decoration is in the fashionable French style of the 1490s and in the dedication the name of Henry VII of England has been substituted by hand for that of Charles VIII of France.